Someone Special

by
Marilee Zdenek

WORD BOOKS
PUBLISHER
WACO, TEXAS

Photographed in Israel
by Marilee Zdenek

Books by Marilee Zdenek
SOMEONE SPECIAL
and in collaboration with Marge Champion
CATCH THE NEW WIND
GOD IS A VERB

For Al

Foreword

Mary, of Nazareth . . . do you know her? She plays such a major role in the unfolding of the Christ story, and yet we know her so little.

But this is a book that brings Mary to life. Fragmentary biblical passages are combined with "sanctified imagination" to provide a new perspective on the humanity of the mother of God. To read it once is to catch a glimpse of a strong, sensitive woman with wide-ranging feelings that run deep and thoughts that are crisp and penetrating. To read it twice is to know Mary better than you know most of your closest friends.

But this is perhaps even more a book about emotion. It deals with Mary's fear and joy, Joseph's rage and compassion, Jesus' loneliness and love, and we understand these intense feelings more intimately and discriminatingly than ever before because through poetry a profound theory of emotion is developed. Every page throbs with the theme: God gave you the capacity to feel. Know abundant life by experiencing all your feelings right to their edges.

So, this is a book about Mary and Joseph and Jesus and John and their most intimate inner living. It is a series of tender, caring, realistic portraits of Jesus' family. And though his mother is on stage, the Savior himself pervades every page.

Neil C. Warren, Dean
Graduate School of Psychology
Fuller Theological Seminary

The world knows her by many names: Blessed Virgin, Holy Mother, Mother of God, the Virgin Mary, or the mother of Jesus. We have seen her on pedestals, heard accolades in her name, marveled at her specialness. But many of us have felt out of touch with her humanity. The scholars say she was thirteen or so, that day the angel came. What was she really like—that young Jewish girl, Mary of Nazareth?

Part I.

At the age of thirteen,
pregnant with the special child of God,
Mary visits the home of her cousin, Elizabeth,
in the village of Bethlehem.

Why Was I Chosen?

Why was I chosen? How can it be,
    that God in His wisdom would ask—
      such commitment of me?

I look around me, only to see
    so many more worthy than I—
      why has He chosen me?

One special evening, God sent the dove,
to touch me and fill me with joy—
Oh! I trembled with love.

Mountains may crumble, noon sky turn black,
whatever may happen I know—
I will never turn back!

I'm not afraid for the Lord is with me,
I'm not afraid for the Lord is here,

holding
 and leading
  and guiding
   and keeping me near.

Oh, but Elizabeth, I was afraid! I trembled when the angel spoke my name. I felt like God himself was calling me and I was so frightened, I fell to the ground and covered my face. But the voice of the angel was gentle and his words were tender, consoling me and telling me not to be afraid for the Lord was with me. He said that I would become pregnant and have a son—someone more special than any child has ever been before.

I protested and said, "But how can that be, for I am a virgin!" And then, Elizabeth, I was so bewildered—he told me that the Holy Spirit would come upon me and the power of God overshadow me and the child from my womb would be Holy and his name called Jesus.

When my fear had passed, the joy in my heart was more than words can say, for how can there be words for what others have never known? And how can I speak of unearthly feelings in earthly terms?

The angel spoke of you, Elizabeth, and I wanted to come to you and tell you of the wonderful things our Lord is doing. But first, of course, I went to Joseph, for it is only right that he should be the first to know of this miracle.

I told Joseph, just as I now told you. He
stared at me as if this were some strange tale
that defied belief. Watching his face,
suddenly drawn and pained, I watched the
doubt overtake all the trust that once he
placed in me. I told him this child was
conceived by the Holy Spirit—he looked at
me as if I had broken every bond between us.

He seemed at first as if a sword had pierced
his soul. And the agony on his face was so
intense, there was no way that I could ease
that pain or reassure him of my love.

I watched the sorrow in his eyes change—in
moments change from grief to anger. My
words could not undo the path his thoughts
had taken. He felt the pain that any man
would feel, believing the woman he trusted
and loved—the woman whose hand he
had never so much as touched—could play
him false.

Elizabeth, I wept—and he as well. Though
my tears were for him, his were in anger
and reproach.

He said he would not go through with the
marriage. He said he would break the
promise of our families and take a bride
more worthy of his trust.

But even in his rage, there soon came
compassion and concern for me. He knew
the pain that would be mine at the hands of
the people if they thought I had been so
dishonored. He could not turn me out to the
village—mark me with that shame. He
began to seek another way of privately
undoing his involvement.

I asked him then to think of how he had
known me—to consider the modesty of my
ways and the protectiveness of my parents—
and to consider again the angel.

"Angels!" he said. "I have never seen
an angel!"

I reminded him of Sara and of Hannah,
and of how angels came to them, telling them
of miracles that were to come from
their wombs—great prophets to be brought
forth from their own bodies. But he said that
was different. That seemed to him somewhat
less a miracle than what I claimed.

And that is true. Never has God so honored
a woman. Still, I know that this honor will
not save me from one thorn that life may hold.
Though I bear the Christ Child, God
will not save me from sorrow. Already it
has begun.

It is not an easy thing (though it is an
exalting thing!). It is not an easy thing to
bear the Son of God in my womb.

I said so to Joseph. He told me that he must
go alone to pray, to think this through,
to decide what was the right thing for him
to do.

And he left me.

That night, I kept my own counsel. I spoke
not to my father nor my mother. Sisters and
brothers slept, huddled close in the cold
room. I alone kept vigil through the night.

Unknown to them, I laid my hopes upon the
will of God, and waited.

How Very Much I Love Him

I cannot sleep, I worry so,
With anxious thoughts I sit alone
And dream of him and of our love
And wonder if he will really go
And wonder if he will ever know
How very much I love him.

Such dreadful thoughts come to my mind,
Tormenting thoughts of fearful lies,
Recurrent thoughts of losing him—
Of never once even touching him.
All through my tears how I long to say
How very much I love him.

There are no words that I can say
To change his mind to make him stay,
To make him see I need him so.
What will I do if he really goes—
If he should leave and still not know
How very much I love him.

In spite of all the things he said
I know he cares, I know he must.
Beneath the sound of angry words,
I'm sure he loves me, I'm sure he does,
I'm sure he knows, he must believe
How very much I love him.

Miracles happen—
    I know that it's true,
        surely our love is meant to be,
        surely our love is right to be,
O God!
    Surely our love
        has been destined by You!

And surely it was so. As evening gave way to the dawn, Joseph returned. All that night I had stayed awake praying that he would come back to me—believing, yet not daring to believe, that my prayers would be answered.

What agony it was to have to stand there and wait until he spoke first to my father, asking permission to talk with me, and then to my mother, showing courtesy and respect.

All the while, my heart was racing with excitement to hear from his lips the message that I read in his eyes.

At last we were able to speak together; our voices whispered in one corner of the room, while my sisters and brothers tried to overhear what was none of their business to know!

Joseph told me then, how the angel came to him in the night, reminding him of the prophecy in Isaiah, where a virgin would conceive a son and the child would be uniquely of God.

The angel told Joseph that I am the virgin of whom Isaiah spoke—and the child that I bear is God's own Son. It is the will of God that Joseph take me as his wife and adopt this child to raise with all the love and tenderness that he would feel toward his own son.

So it is as I prayed, as God had planned all along: Joseph will be God's chosen father for the Holy Son.

I do wonder about this child, Elizabeth. How strange it seems that a boy who will grow up to be ruler of all Israel should be born in so ordinary a city as Nazareth and in so humble a place as Joseph's house. I should have thought that God would want him to be born in the Holy City of Jerusalem.

Still, I will make our home as lovely as I can, choosing the warmest corner of the room to give him birth. The best of midwives must be chosen and there will be fine oil to bathe him as soon as he is born. I hope Joseph's father won't be hurt that the baby won't be named for him. But Jesus is a lovely name!

As he grows, he will be much like other
children, I should think—learning slowly to
crawl and to walk, to run in the hills of
Galilee. He must learn, in the natural order
of things, how to talk, to sing, to sit in the
temple and learn from the rabbis.

I will make toys of clay and Joseph will carve
a dreidel for him to spin. I wonder if he will
play in the flowered hillsides like my
brothers—and help me with the chores.

When he's older, will he like working with
his father in the shop? Will he like to fish the
waters of Galilee, or tend the flocks of sheep
upon the hills?

What manner of child will this be, Elizabeth?
Uniquely of God, and yet, so totally,
completely human—

If he runs, surely he must grow weary.

If he cuts his finger—will he bleed?

Someone Special

I will sing to my child, I will dream with my son,
I will hold him and rock him and show him my love.
We will laugh, we will play, we will dance through the day
With a prayer in our hearts for the world God has made.

I can just see him now as he works in the shop,
How his arms must be strong for the work there is hard.
See him now walking tall, reaching out as he goes
To the people and teaching how God loves them all.

I can just see him now as he walks through the town
Loving people and telling them what God's about—
Reaching out to a child, reaching out with a smile
As he touches and heals them and turns them about.

Oh, he's someone special,
    Someone special,   He's someone special,
      That is so easy to see,   Someone special,
                    That much is certain to me.

I can just see him now as he moves from the crowd
To a place that is lonely, a place that is hard.
Oh, he seems so alone for his friends have all gone
And I feel in my soul how the sky has turned dark!

Still, I know in my heart that the Lord has his plan—
He will rise up and be the great savior of man.
As I go on my way I will not be alone,
He·will be by my side—he will call me his own.

Oh, he's someone special,
   Someone special,   *He's someone special,*
    That is so easy to see,   *Someone special,*
                      That much is certain to me.

Part II.

An elderly woman now,
    Mary lives in the home of the Apostle John,
in the village of Ephesus.

Preparing the Passover dinner,
    her thoughts turn toward the past.

And he really was special. He was all I could have wished for—and more. Even from the beginning, I could see that. I don't know why others didn't see it from the start—it was so obvious to Joseph and to me. The sound of his laughter was just a little more joyful—his eyes, just a little more aware. And how loving was the touch of his hand upon my face.

Dear Lord! Here I am reminiscing again, when there is work to be done. The holidays are upon us and there is not time for thinking about the past. How many years has it been? Fifty-two? Fifty-three, since the angel came. Elizabeth is gone now, and Joseph . . . and my son.

Everything turned out so differently than I had imagined. Even from the beginning, Lord, when I realized that my son—*Your* son, was to be born in a stable! Well, that wasn't at all the way I thought you would have planned it. Still, you never were one to do things the way people might have thought. And as it turned out, the stable wasn't such a bad place for having a baby after all. Once I got accustomed to the idea.

Now, here I go again, daydreaming instead of cooking. Soon all the family will be gathering—hungry and anxious for the Seder to begin. I am almost ready; the house has been rid of flour and the dishes have been changed for the Passover. The soup is made—the lamb is on the fire—but there is still more cooking to be done.

Come, Lord, bless me with the spirit of Your joy as I work.

Kitchen Prayer

Praise God, alleluia, alleluia, praise God.
Praise God, alleluia, alleluia, praise God.

For the onions and the matzah and the celery and the stock,
For the herbs and for the spices and the chicken in the pot.
For the fire and for the hearth, for the kettle and the spoon,
I will praise you, I will praise you, all afternoon.

Praise God, alleluia, alleluia, praise God.
Praise God, alleluia, alleluia, praise God.

For the table and the flowers and the candles and the wine,
For the nuts and for the apples and the parsley and the lamb,
For my sons and for their wives and the children every one—
I will praise you, I will praise you, 'til day is done.

Praise God, alleluia, alleluia, praise God.
Praise God, alleluia, alleluia, praise God.

$\mathcal{W}$ho is it? . . . Who's there? John! John, welcome home! Thank God you're here—but so thin! You are working much too hard and not eating properly at all. You must take better care of yourself! Come in, come in. Sit down while I fix you something to eat. . . . Nonsense—the Passover feast will not begin until sundown and there is still an hour of daylight in the sky. Have a bowl of soup at least, not enough to spoil your appetite. How thin you are, John! . . . Come, you can talk later, first eat.

I have been so anxious for news of you and of all that's going on in Jerusalem. When you didn't come earlier in the day, I was afraid you wouldn't be home in time for the Seder. It would have been just like Paul to keep all of you tied up in the Council in Jerusalem over the holidays!

Paul just isn't a family man at heart. I don't
think he realizes how important it is that
you and the others—especially the married
ones—should be back with your families over
the Passover. . . . Oh, he does . . . well, I'm
glad he agrees.

Is the soup good? . . . Do you think it needs
more salt? . . . No? I don't think so either.

Was Peter there at the Council? . . . Is he
going to Rome? Well, if he goes, I hope he
comes first through Ephesus so I can have
a good visit with him. You boys do push
yourselves, not getting enough rest, working
all the time.

Even Jesus took time off, you know. He used to get into Matthew's boat and sail off toward Tiberias when the crowds wouldn't let him rest. I think it would be well for you to remember that, when you go pushing beyond your endurance—and not eating properly besides. Would you like more soup now? Not just a little? . . . No, no, I wouldn't want to spoil your appetite tonight! This Passover feast will surely be the best in years.

Tell me now, did you get much accomplished at the Council? . . . Really! Well, Paul has always been a bit outspoken. I like a man who speaks his mind, but he has never been one to soften his opinions, I've noticed.

I do worry about Paul. I heard what happened in Lystra—they actually stoned him and left him for dead! He takes no caution, none at all! Oh, John, how I do worry about each one of these men. I understand the commitment—I share it as well. But still I fear the day when the price will be paid and another life martyred to the faith.

When I look at you, I see my son— something about your eyes is so much the same. Did I not worry about him every day he preached? I heard the things he said to the rich and to the powerful. Men are not so quick to change their ways! I saw their anger grow. He knew, better than I, what was to happen. He could have turned back, you know, at any time. He could have chosen to save himself. I didn't understand at first, how high the price would be for him to be the Savior of the world. It was not an easy thing to give him up—not even to fulfill that destiny.

I see you sitting there and I remember when
he sat in our home, waiting for the Seder, just
like you—his eyes sparkling, just like yours.
I can almost hear the sound of his laughter
and remember the way he played with the
children—lifting them high into the air.

How strong his arms were, from the hard,
rugged work in Joseph's shop. I can see
his hands—callused and rough—but with
one touch of those workman's hands, the
lame could walk and the blind could see.

I remember when he was a boy, what a
strong-willed son he was—running off and
giving me such a fright! Well, I didn't
understand at all in those days. I was always
trying to protect him, even then. He never let
me, though—even when he was a little
boy, he was always climbing on the highest
walls, always telling me not to worry.

Not to worry! O my son . . . my boy . . .

My Son, My Boy

My son,
My boy,
Will I ever stop missing the sound of your voice?
Will I ever stop wanting to touch you?
Just touch you.

It's been a long time,
Such a long time;
The village has stayed much the same.
The places you played
When you were a child
Are still full of children,
Of laughter and cries.
The walls where you climbed
Are still standing strong
And the friends that I see
Just keep speaking of you
All the time.

It's been a long time,
Such a long time,
Still people are so good to me.
Your friends come around
To see that I'm well,
To bring me some laughter,
To bring me some smiles.
Your brothers are kind,
They care for me so.
But no one can heal
This great longing I feel in my soul.

My son,
My boy,
Will I ever stop missing the sound of your voice?
Will I ever stop wanting to touch you?
Just—touch you.

John, forgive me, I shouldn't go on like this.
It is the season of the year, even after all
this time—the coming of Passover makes
the feelings surface. Please don't be so
concerned. I'm fine—just fine.

Of course, the Holy Spirit comforts me—
how could I have survived what happened
had that not been true!

The Holy Spirit comforts me, but never
takes away my humanity. He wipes the tears
from my eyes, but never does he forbid the
tears to come.

Nor would I have it so. How easy the young would have life to be! John, I would not want to lose touch with any one of the emotions of life—even those deep feelings that cause me pain.

If I could not mourn, how deeply could I love? If I could not cry, how hollow would be the sound of my laughter!

Don't you remember how Jesus wept when
Lazarus died? He wept, not for his friend, but
for himself—for the loss of that friendship—
for the years of loneliness that he would feel
until they were reunited in heaven.

Now, if Jesus was not afraid of these feelings,
neither should I be. Oh, I have heard men
say that, because of their faith, they are
always happy. Well, that was not true of
their Lord!

Jesus was sometimes angry, sometimes lonely, sometimes even afraid.

Oh, there was great joy about him—but this joy was not at the expense of other emotions.

I do wonder about people who want life to be other than human.

As for me, I've tasted a little from every cup
and grown through the struggles. I have loved
until I ached from loving, and wept until my
heart was sick of tears. I have known life in all
of its complexity—and looking back, I would
not undo one moment, if I could.

Let my tears come when they will—for then
God sends His Spirit, bringing comfort
beyond what man can ever give, and peace
so complete it defies all understanding.

Mary's Psalm

Giver of life, creator of all that is lovely,
                teach me to sing the words to your song;
I want to feel the music of living
                and not fear the sad songs
                but from them make new songs
                composed of both laughter and tears.

Teach me to dance to sounds of your world and your people,
                I want to move in rhythm with your plan,
Help me to try to follow your leading
                to risk even falling
                to rise and keep trying
                because you are leading the dance.

Holy Spirit,
        live in me;
                Holy Spirit,
                        set me free.

Almighty God, you bless me with life that's abundant,
  I feel your love, surrounding me each day.
You are the source of all that is lovely,
  how great is your goodness,
  how tender your caring,
  how simple the song that you gave.

Holy Spirit,
    live in me;
        Holy spirit,
          set me free.

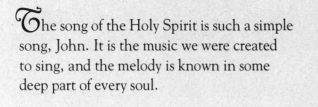

The song of the Holy Spirit is such a simple song, John. It is the music we were created to sing, and the melody is known in some deep part of every soul.

Jesus taught the words, and waits now to hear the singing.

I can just hear him now, telling us to put God
first and not to worship power and money.
He speaks of loving all men as our brothers
and caring for the poor and the lonely.

And the love song he sings for us is so simple.
The words speak of forgiveness for all the
destructive choices we make; the words speak
of acceptance, for he knows our hearts and
loves us in spite of our weakness.

He came that we might have life, and have it more abundantly.

And he died, and rose from the dead, so that those who love him would have the assurance of eternal life.

Oh, he's someone special,
  someone special,
    that is so easy to see–

He's someone special,
  someone special,
    that much is certain to me.